BLACK WATCH

by the same author

GAGARIN WAY
THE STRAITS
ON TOUR

The National Theatre of Scotland's

Black Watch

GREGORY BURKE

ff

faber and faber

First published in 2007
by Faber and Faber Limited
3 Queen Square, London WC1N 3AU
Published in the United States by Faber and Faber Inc.
an affiliate of Farrar, Straus and Giroux LLC, New York

Typeset by Country Setting, Kingsdown, Kent CT14 8ES
Printed in England by Bookmarque, Croydon, Surrey

A CIP record for this book
is available from the British Library

ISBN 978-0-571-23817-0

2 4 6 8 10 9 7 5 3 1

Contents

Author's Note

During the rehearsals for *Black Watch*, a former Regimental Sergeant Major of the Regiment gave the actors the benefit of both two hundred and sixty-seven years of parade ground insults, and of the particular attention the Regiment pays to what a layman might find trivial. The exact way to wear your tam-o'-shanter. How to make your combats hang over your boots in just the right way. The impulse to turn as much of the world as possible into an acronym. But mostly what he taught them about was pride. To take a pride in yourself. To take a pride in what you are doing. To take a pride in your appearance. To take a pride in what you represent. When the actors first mastered a piece of marching, he took them outside and made them march in the street: he was proud of them and he wanted other people to see what they could do. A couple of days later, one of the actors – whose first professional job this is after drama school – told me that if the acting doesn't work out he thinks he might join the army for a couple of years. To me this was indicative of the seductive nature of surrendering yourself to an institution that has refined its appeal to the male psyche's yearning for a strong identity.

The Black Watch, like any military unit, has to carve out its own identity. It has to see itself and its members as special. Their glorious victories and defeats are drummed into recruits from the day they enter basic training. There's the Pipes and Drums who played at JFK's funeral and tour the world. There's even a troop, or maybe that should be troupe, of Highland dancers who are riflemen during the day and sword dancers when occasion demands. The army defines these things as force-multipliers. The stream of recruits continues because there is a cachet to be had from serving in the Black Watch, the oldest Highland regiment.

They call it the Golden Thread, the connection that runs through the history of the regiment since its formation. Even today, in our supposedly fractured, atomised society, the regiment exists on a different plane. In Iraq there were lads serving alongside their fathers. There were groups of friends from even the smallest communities. Four from the former fishing village of St Monans. Seven from the former mining village of High Valleyfield. Dozens from Dundee and Dunfermline, Kirkcaldy and Perth. Friends and family. Uncles, brothers, cousins, fathers, sons, schoolmates. The army does best in areas of the country which the Ministry of Defence describes as having 'settled communities'. As an estate agent's euphemism it isn't quite up there with 'needs buyers with imagination', but I think we know what they are hinting at. The army does not recruit well in London or any other big city. Metropolitanism and multiculturalism are not the things that are welded into a cohesive fighting force. Fighting units tend to be more at home with homogeneity. Not that there aren't other nationalities in the Black Watch. There are Fijians and Zimbabweans, even a few Glaswegians. However, the central core of the regiment has always been the heartland of Perthshire, Fife, Dundee and Angus. It both represents and reflects those communities.

The Black Watch is a tribe. It is also, overwhelmingly, a working-class institution. As much a part of the social history of Scotland as mining, shipbuilding or fishing. Indeed, soldiering, like banking, is arguably the only significant indigenous industry to have lasted into the twenty-first century. Whether it lasts much longer, now all the Scottish regiments have been amalgamated into one single 'super regiment', remains to be seen. When the clans of Scotland used to fight they would have people who stood in front of the soldiers and recited the names of their ancestors. In the end, soldiers don't fight for Britain or for the government or for Scotland. They fight for their regiment. Their company. Their platoon. And for their mates.

This was the first time I had worked on a large-scale piece of theatre. When I began I didn't realise quite how much of a theatrical business the army is. Why it hadn't occurred to me before, I don't know. After all, many people's sole experience of the Edinburgh Festival takes place at the Military Tattoo. As we worked, and as new ideas and possibilities revealed themselves, the scope of the piece grew. These possibilities could not have been exploited without the resources of the National Theatre of Scotland, the dedication of Vicky Featherstone and the creative team, and the ambition of John Tiffany's artistic vision. David Loyn, the BBC reporter embedded with the regiment at Dogwood, also contributed valuable insights into the deployment and the difficulties facing those on the ground. The cast took everything that was thrown at them – even the fact that we didn't have a final script until the previews – without complaint. It was John who had the unenviable task of welding together the strands of script, music and movement into a cohesive whole. That he managed it at all – and my hunch is that booze and Nurofen played a crucial supporting role – is a testament to his, and Vicky's, determination to make the National Theatre of Scotland a success. We're lucky to have them here.

Gregory Burke, February 2007

Director's Note

In August 2005, a couple of months after I started working at the National Theatre of Scotland, I attended a cycle of plays at the King's Theatre in Edinburgh as part of the International Festival. The cycle was produced by the Galway-based Druid Theatre Company and consisted of all six of J. M. Synge's plays performed by the same company of actors over nine hours with breaks for sustenance. It was a truly amazing experience to sit and watch the entire dramatic output of one brilliant playwright. As a celebration of the achievements of Irish theatre, it felt truly national.

I got to thinking about the role of NTS in terms of the history of Scottish theatre, and how we could honour and rouse its traditions. There have been, and continue to be, many great dramatists producing great plays over the years. Major revivals of Scottish classics along with world premieres will always have a strong presence in our programme. But the plays are not the whole story.

Fuelled by variety, visual art, music and a deep love of storytelling, Scotland's artists have created a form of theatre that is as significant and vital as its written drama. It features narration, song, movement, stand-up comedy, film, politics and, above all, an urgent need to connect with its audience. It is often contemporaneous with world events and issues, although never dry and academic, and therefore deeply relevant and bound to the time in which it is created. It is a distinct form of theatre of which Scotland can be very proud.

It is a tradition that has been fired by, and has found expression in, the work of a great number of theatre companies and artists: John McGrath and 7:84 changed the face of Scottish theatre with *The Cheviot, the Stag and the Black, Black Oil*, which encompassed two hundred years of Scottish history from the Clearances in the eighteenth century to the discovery of North Sea oil in the seventies; Gerry Mulgrew and Communicado collaborated with Liz Lochhead and Edwin Morgan to create visceral and riotous shows such as *Mary Queen of Scots Got Her Head Chopped Off* and *Cyrano de Bergerac*; Bill Bryden told the story of dying industry with a great demotic energy in *The Ship*, performed in the Harland and Wolff shipyard in Govan. All these pieces of theatre used cabaret, spectacle, passion and honesty to communicate with their audiences. It is these productions, among others, that were the inspiration behind the ambition of *Black Watch*.

This ambition resulted in a development and rehearsal process that was unfamiliar to me, Greg Burke and the creative team. For the most part we were making it up as we went along. At the end of 2004, as one of the first things she did as Artistic Director of NTS, Vicky Featherstone asked Greg to keep an eye on the story of the Black Watch, who had just returned to Scotland from Camp Dogwood. When I joined the company in April 2005, Greg had discovered some fascinating stories with real dramatic potential, so we decided to programme the piece in our inaugural year as a 'highly physical piece of political theatre'. I told Greg *not* to go away and write a fictional drama set in Iraq, but that instead we should try and tell the 'real' stories of the soldiers in their own words. This led to Greg interviewing a group of Black Watch lads in a Fife pub over a couple of months (thanks to our researcher Sophie Johnston), all of whom had just left the regiment. I knew that I wanted to perform the piece in a space in which we could create our own version of the Tattoo, with seating banks down either side of an esplanade. This we found in Edinburgh, in an old drill hall near the Castle that was being used as a car park by the university. For the first time as a director, and through nobody's fault but my own, I was going into rehearsals without a script. All we had were the interviews, some traditional Black Watch songs and the dimensions of the drill hall.

Luckily Greg had been secretly writing some fictional scenes set in Dogwood and these made a powerful contrast with the pub interviews. We soon had material from Steven Hoggett,

Associate Director (Movement), who was working with the actors on a 'letters from home' sequence and brought in a Regimental Sergeant Major to teach us parade marches, and Davey Anderson, Associate Director (Music), who was creating radical new arrangements of the Black Watch songs. We also had fantastic support from Sarah Alford-Smith, our Stage Manager, who created a twenty-first-century rehearsal environment with internet access, DVD players and video cameras, and who, along with the actors, collated a goldmine of news reports, radio extracts, documentaries, political speeches, statistics and visual references. Even with all this material it still wasn't clear to us whether we had a piece of theatre that would communicate anything to an audience. We continued not to know until the first night in Edinburgh. Then it became apparent that there was a real connection being made and that we were telling a story that the audience desperately wanted to hear.

When it came to remounting *Black Watch* and we started talking about publishing the text, we all agreed that we wanted to produce something that would reflect this process and give a sense of the experience of watching the production that couldn't be understood from the words alone. Therefore, I have written production notes, which are distinguished from the text by being indented betwen rules in a different font, and chosen production photographs to correspond with moments and sequences that weren't spoken but were still trying to communicate something to an audience.

Mainly, what I really want to communicate here is that the ambition behind *Black Watch* was to create a piece of theatre that would harness the energy of a tradition of Scottish theatre and a long line of artists, and that this tradition is fundamental to our future as theatre-makers.

John Tiffany, February 2007

[NATIONAL THEATRE OF SCOTLAND]

Black Watch has been described in the press as a cultural landmark of the twenty-first century (*Sunday Herald*, 4 March). A lofty claim indeed, but it is only once in a lifetime that a piece of theatre is created which celebrates the vibrancy and possibility of the art form with every second of its performance, which explodes something we are collectively struggling to understand – in this case the Iraq War – and provides a visceral resonance which permeates universally. *Black Watch* is that piece of theatre. That it exists at all is testament to the wonderful people who made it and to the stories the soldiers communicated to us, but also to something which could be another cultural landmark of the twenty-first century – the National Theatre of Scotland. *Black Watch* sums up what we are and what we want to be. We have no building, which means we can create theatre without walls. We work in partnership to find the appropriate co-producers and theatres for our work to have maximum impact on our audience. Paradoxically, that *Black Watch* remains so urgent is not something to be celebrated. Only this morning on the news I heard that nine US soldiers were killed as were thirty Iraqi civilians in a bomb in Baghdad.

Since our programme burst onto the theatre scene in February 2006 with its opening production *Home*, which took place simultaneously in ten different regions in Scotland from Shetland and Stornoway in the north to Dumfries and Galloway in the south, we have produced many different pieces of theatre in over sixty different locations. Although *Black Watch* has taken us all by storm, we have a fantastic body of other work too which has exceeded all our expectations. I urge you to visit our website to give you a flavour of these.

Everything to which we aspire is about challenging the notion of what theatre can achieve, about enabling creative professionals and participants to take risks and be innovative, about trying to do things flexibly and out of our comfort zones to create experiences for audiences which merit the creation of a cultural institution in an international world in the twenty-first century. As far as we can, we want to create environments for artists to flourish, for their voices to come through – and for us to trust that through them we can see our complex world in a different way.

Black Watch started as an assignment – I asked Gregory Burke to follow the story of the soon-to-be-amalgamated Black Watch Regiment in 2004. He was of course already doing this, which is why he was the right person for the job. We have about ten assignments a year where we ask playwrights and artists to follow something – anything from huge stories to fleeting moments – not needing to know where they will end.

From this work, Greg and John Tiffany created *Black Watch* through a series of workshops and research sessions. They achieved this thanks to a stunning and fearless creative team, comprising Steven Hoggett, Davey Anderson, Laura Hopkins, Jessica Brettle and Gareth Fry; and thanks to the tireless trust and brilliance of the cast. The first time it was a leap into the unknown. Doing it again has created another set of challenges, but I want to thank everyone at NTS who has worked so hard to bring this back.

If the non-building-based model of this National Theatre of Scotland can create something so universal, so powerful and so pertinent, we genuinely do have the opportunity here to create a cultural landmark. Not a monument to the past, but rather a breathing, flexible, challenging and bold movement for the future.

Vicky Featherstone, Artistic Director

www.nationaltheatrescotland.com
0141 221 0970

Black Watch was first performed on Saturday 5 August 2006 at the Drill Hall, Forest Hill, Edinburgh. The original cast included Jordan Young (Rossco) and Paul Higgins (Writer and Sergeant). The 2007 revival cast, in order of appearance, was as follows:

Cammy Brian Ferguson
Granty Paul Rattray
Rossco Henry Pettigrew
Macca David Colvin
Stewarty Ali Craig
Nabsy Nabil Stuart
Writer *and* **Sergeant** Tom Smith
Fraz Emun Elliott
Kenzie Ryan Fletcher
Officer Peter Forbes

All additional parts played by members of the company

Director John Tiffany
Associate Director (*Movement*) Steven Hoggett
Associate Director (*Music*) Davey Anderson
Set Design Laura Hopkins
Sound Design Gareth Fry
Lighting Design Colin Grenfell
Costume Design and Wardrobe Supervisor Jessica Brettle
Video Design Leo Warner and Mark Grimmer for
    Fifty Nine Productions Ltd
Assistant Director Andrew Panton
Company Stage Manager Carrie Hutcheon
Company Stage Manager (*Rehearsals*) Ruth Crighton
Deputy Stage Manager Sarah Alford-Smith

Assistant Stage Manager Fiona Kennedy
Lighting Supervisor Maria Bechaalani
Sound Supervisor Andrew Elliott
Audio-Visual Technician Kenny Christie
Stage Technician Jane Seymour
Technician David Graham
Wardrobe Assistant Christine Dove

Thanks also to:

Lorna Brain, Elaine Coyle, Ali Currie, Louise Davidson,
Jim Ferguson, Fiona Fraser, Lesley Fraser, Kirsty Glover,
John Humphrys, Ewan Hunter, Sophie Johnston,
Sandy Leishman, David Loyn, Jon Meggat, Thomas Moles,
Kevin Murray, Victoria Paulo, P. J. Pendlebury, Brendan
Savage, Ros Steen, Duncan Stone; and to all at the Traverse
Theatre, the University of Edinburgh, the Black Watch
Regimental Museum, J&B Scenery, Scottish Opera, Torbay
Costume Hire, Mitcorp, the Erdington Group, the RSAMD,
the Royal Lyceum Theatre and Scottish Youth Theatre

Characters

Cammy

Granty

Rossco

Stewarty

Macca

Nabsy

Writer

Fraz

Kenzie

Sergeant

Officer

BLACK WATCH

Production notes are indented between rules
in this sans serif font.

TATTOO

The audience enter a large space with seating banks down either side creating an esplanade flanked by four scaffold towers. Screens are hung from each of the towers which are used to give a sense of location (sport in the pub scenes and military CCTV in Camp Dogwood). Bagpipe and drum Tattoo music blares and moving saltire lights sweep the floor, walls and ceiling. The music builds to a climax as the voice-over begins.

Voice-Over Good evening, ladies and gentlemen, and welcome to the unique setting of the Edinburgh Drill Hall. It's almost time for the thrilling moment when the gates swing open. The unforgettable first sight and sound of the massed pipes and drums. Ladies and gentlemen, may we present the Black Watch.

A cannon stops the music as a door at one end of the space creaks open to reveal Cammy, dressed in civvies.

Cammy A'right. Welcome to this story of the Black Watch.

Beat.

At first, I didnay want tay day this.

Beat.

I didnay want tay have tay explain myself tay people ay.

Beat.

See, I think people's minds are usually made up about you if you were in the army.

3

Beat.

They are though ay?

Beat.

They poor fucking boys. They cannay day anything else. They cannay get a job. They get exploited by the army.

Beat.

Well I want you to fucking know. I wanted to be in the army. I could have done other stuff. I'm not a fucking knuckle-dragger.

Pause.

And people's minds are made up about the war that's on the now ay?

Beat.

They are. It's no right. It's illegal. We're just big bullies.

Beat.

Well, we'll need to get fucking used tay it. Bullying's the fucking job. That's what you have a fucking army for.

Music. Granty, Rossco, Stewarty, Macca and Nabsy run on pushing a pool table and carrying pub furniture. We are in a Fife pub on a Sunday afternoon.

PUB I

Cammy So where does it all begin? See, what happened was, this tasty researcher lassie phoned us up ay. She got my name out ay the fucking paper. She phones us up ay and says she's a fucking researcher, a fucking researcher for what? The fucking theatre. Wants tay find out about Iraq. Will I talk tay her?

Beat.

4

I'll talk tay any bird ay. And she was quite nice. And then I met her and like I say she was pretty tasty and ken, you never fucking know ay. Couple ay drinks, couple ay war stories, you dinnay ken where that scene's gonnay end up.

Beat.

Nay fucking luck like, but anyway, then she asks can I speak tay some ay your pals.

Beat.

That's how I got every cunt tay come along ay.

Granty From what he fucking told us we were all getting our cock's sucked by this posh lassie. *(Short, Redley one)*

Rossco She was gagging for a line up from some battle- *(Similar)* hardened Black Watch toby.

Stewarty She was gonnay buy us drink all day and suck our cocks. *(tall blonde)*

Nabsy I'd pit my best gear on. *(Tall dark)*

Cammy And then this cunt fucking appears.

The Writer enters.

Writer Hi.

Cammy A'right.

Granty I thought you said there was a bird coming.

Cammy There is. There is. Is she parking the car?

Writer Who?

Rossco He looks like a poof.

Cammy The lassie?

Macca He does ay.

Cammy The researcher girl?

Writer Sophie?

5

Granty Sophie.

Cammy Aye.

Writer She's not coming.

Cammy No?

Writer No.

Granty She's no coming?

Cammy No.

Granty It's just him?

Cammy Aye.

Granty There's no gonnay be any birds?

Cammy No.

Rossco Fuck it. I'm off.

Granty Me tay.

Writer Does anybody want a drink?

Cammy You buying?

Writer It's on expenses.

Granty All day?

Writer Yes.

Cammy A pint ay Guinness.

Writer Anyone else?

Granty Go on then.

Rossco I think I'll maybe try one.

Stewarty It would be rude not to.

Nabsy Lager.

Macca Same for me.

Writer Do you come here every Sunday?

Cammy Aye.

Rossco Sunday sesh ay.

Granty Watch the football.

Rossco Blether pish.

Cammy What day you want tay know?

Writer What it was like in Iraq.

Cammy What it was fucking like?

Stewarty Go tay fucking Baghdad if you want tay ken what it's like.

Writer No. I'm sorry.

Beat.

What I mean is . . . I want to know about your experience, what it was like for you. For the soldiers. On the ground.

Cammy It wasnay like I thought it was gonnay be. I don't know what the fuck I thought it was gonnay be like, but it wasnay like what it was.

Granty I thought it was gonnay be exciting.

Stewarty It was before it started.

Rossco I thought it was gonnay tell me something about the meaning ay life ay.

Nabsy But he was too busy shooting folk.

Writer So what did it tell you?

Cammy That I didnay want tay be in the army any more.

Rossco Me neither.

Granty None ay us.

7

Gunfire. The Soldiers, Writer and pub disappear.

The surface of the pool table splits open and Fraz and Kenzie emerge from inside dressed in desert combats, berets and red hackles. Over this we hear an extract from the *Today* programme.

John Humphrys The time is ten past eight. There was deep concern, anger indeed, when the news leaked out a few weeks ago that the soldiers of the Black Watch were to be sent north to help out the Americans in Iraq. The area in which they were to be deployed was described here as the 'triangle of death'. So it has turned out for three of them blown up yesterday by a suicide car-bomber. Eight more were injured. The ambush had been carefully planned. Two warrior vehicles were damaged in the first stage of the attack and when other soldiers tried to stage a rescue operation they came under fire from mortar bombs from other insurgents. The dead soldiers will, of course, be mourned, are being mourned. With me are the Defence Secretary, Geoff Hoon, and the leader of the Scottish National Party, Alex Salmond, who says grief will be replaced by something else.

Alex Salmond I think it will give way to a wave of anger as Scotland and the Black Watch families compare and contrast the bravery of our Scottish soldiers with the duplicity and chicanery of the politicians who sent them into this deployment.

John Humphrys Is that anger justified, Mr Hoon?

Geoff Hoon No, it is not, and I'm afraid the leader of the Scottish Nationalists' comments demonstrate clearly there are no depths to which he will not sink to seek – and I can't understand why he does this, I cannot understand why someone should seek to take political advantage about the tragic deaths of three brave men and their interpreter.

Alex Salmond These are professional soldiers, they'll do their job, regardless of the danger, they're among the finest infantry soldiers in the world, but we and I believe that this deployment was political in its nature, we think the request was political, the answer was political, during the American presidential election.

Geoff Hoon He and his colleagues and other Members of Parliament who raise that issue were given absolute assurances by me, by the Prime Minister, by other members of the Government, that there was simply no political motive underlying this request from the United States, that this was a straightforward military request, along military lines of communication to satisfy a specific military task.

(**Alex Salmond** The Black Watch have been sent in to do an impossible job – eight hundred Scottish soldiers are replacing four thousand American marines and we're actually expected to believe that one hundred and thirty thousand American soldiers in Iraq couldn't do that job.)

CAMP INCOMING

Central Iraqi desert, October 2004.

Kenzie D'you think it's got Sky?

Fraz I hope so. We'll be able to watch the news and find out why the fuck we're here.

Kenzie This is fucking pish.

Fraz This isnay in the adverts, ay?

Kenzie Have we actually got tay live here?

Fraz Dinnay worry, it's just till some cunt kills you.

Kenzie What the fuck are we gonnay day here?

    Cammy, Rossco, Stewarty, Granty, Nabsy and Macca enter.

Cammy Your fucking job.

9

Nabsy I thought the Yanks were here?

Rossco Aye, so did I.

Cammy Right. Come on. Let's get a fucking move on. Get the wagon emptied and get sorted out.

Stewarty Get your kit squared away and we can hay a brew.

Cammy We'll hay tay start getting this place fortified. Get fucking sandbags in they windows an that.

Granty The now?

Cammy Aye, the now.

Fraz What for?

Rossco Aye. I was hearing that intelligence reckon they dinnay even ken we're here yet.

> *There are two explosions as mortar bombs land on the camp. Nabsy, Kenzie and Macca dive for cover. Cammy, Grant, Rossco, Stewarty and Fraz stand unmoved.*

Cammy That got youse fucking moving.

Rossco Fraz, you'll need tay get these cunts sorted out.

> *There is another explosion.*

Fraz Welcome to Camp Dogwood.

Granty In beautiful Babil province.

Cammy Ancient home ay Babylon.

Rossco Birthplace ay civilisation.

> *Another mortar lands. This time very close, making them all dive for cover.*

Cammy Twenty-four-hour beach facilities.

Granty A scorpion in every tent.

Fraz Friendly locals.

Rossco Your home for the next six months.

Another explosion.

Macca Six fucking months?

Nabsy I thought they said we were gonnay be home by Christmas?

Cammy You didnay believe that shite, did you?

Stewarty This is the fucking army we're talking about here.

The Sergeant enters.

Sergeant What are youse fucking daying?

Another explosion.

Cammy Taking cover, Sergeant.

Sergeant Taking cover?

Cammy Someone's firing . . .

Another explosion.

Mortars. Light. If I'm no mistaken.

Sergeant They're just saying hello. You fucking shitebags.

Granty You'd think they would have fucking let us get unpacked before they attacked us.

Fraz Cheeky bastards.

Sergeant What, have you no read *jihadi* infantry manual number four-four-seven-nine-one-six-five-three?

Another explosion.

Inshallah!

Beat.

The infidel shall be attacked at the rising ay the sun and at its setting. And when he unpacks his decadent western sunblock.

Another explosion.

Allah akhbar.

My darling, you said in my last e-mail I sounded worried? Well, we are here in Dogwood and the task does look quite challenging.

At least our mission is now clear. The Americans, gearing up for an assault on Fallujah, have asked for an armoured battalion to take up blocking positions in the desert south-east of the city. Our mission will be to cut off the insurgents' lines of communication and police the terrorist rat runs out to Baghdad.

Our orders are to apply our own tactics and, in contrast to the 'firepower and force protection first' style of the Americans, get out among the local population and win hearts and minds.

We have a limited intelligence assessment of the threat we face and there has been no coalition presence for a month prior to our deployment. We also haven't had enough time to assess the situation here and develop appropriate tactics, techniques and procedures to deal with a much tougher environment. These will have to be developed as the operation progresses. In other words, we will have to make it up as we go along.

There have been so many hacks and TV crews buzzing around us on the way north, I expect every lunatic terrorist for miles around to descend on us like bees to honey. We've already had a pretty warm welcome.

So thanks to all the prevarication at ministerial level about the most media-friendly moment for the deployment to be announced, the chances are the insurgents will know more about us than we do about them. I wouldn't be surprised if they had been in and mapped our positions before we got here. I hope the government knows what it has got us into. I am not sure they fully understand the risks.

The jocks are well and are coming at it with their usual gallows humour but the marines we have replaced here have

taken nine dead and nearly two hundred wounded since July.
I hope we do better.

NEW BOYS

Fraz and Cammy are relaxing with their trousers rolled down over their boots. Fraz gets a bottle of water from the back of the wagon.

Fraz You wanting one?

Cammy I'm fine.

Fraz (*opens his water and drinks*) Where the fuck day they get this stuff?

Cammy It's no fucking Evian, that's for fucking sure.

Fraz How's your book?

Cammy 'S not bad. Shame I'm just about finished it.

Beat.

He was here, you know?

Fraz Lawrence ay Arabia?

Cammy Right fucking here.

Fraz (*looks around*) Lucky bastard ay.

Cammy Aye.

Fraz And what did he do, when he was here?

Cammy What did he do?

Fraz Aye. What's it about?

Cammy It's . . . eh, well, he kinday . . .

Fraz You dinnay ken what it's about?

Cammy I ken it's *The Seven Pillars ay Wisdom*, but it's hard tay tell what it's about when there's only half ay it ay.

13

Fraz It's the *Three and a Half Pillars ay Wisdom*?

Cammy That's the trouble way paperbacks ay. They arenay designed tay stand up tay the rigours ay expeditionary soldiering.

Fraz D'you ken who's got the other half?

Cammy Some'dy in Five Platoon, I think he said.

Fraz You gonnay get it off him?

Cammy Fuck aye. (*Pause.*) Where are Five, anyway?

Fraz Fuck knows. Driving about somewhere trying tay find the cunts that are mortaring us.

Cammy Have we still not found them?

There is an explosion in the distance.

Fraz Apparently not.

Cammy Well, I hope they're back soon – (*Holds up the book.*) because now I ken how it finishes I'm dying tay ken what the fuck the cunt was daying here in the first place.

Fraz Is it like the film?

Cammy What?

Fraz The book? Is it like the film? Ay *Lawrence ay Arabia*?

Cammy Is it fuck.

Fraz I bet it's nowhere near as good as the fucking film.

Cammy No.

Fraz Never is, is it?

Cammy Never.

Fraz Do you think they'll make a film about this war?

Cammy They fucking better. I didnay fucking join the army for it no tay get immortalised on the big fucking screen.

Fraz You dinnay think it'll be too fucking boring?

14

Cammy Maybe. (*Pause.*) I'll do it my fucking self. Film it on fucking Kinghorn beach. Who'll fucking know? *Sweating Wayout Moving.*

Beat.

That's what I'll call it.

Rossco and Kenzie enter. Rossco is carrying a piece of paper.

Cammy What the fuck are you daying?

Rossco Battlefield skills.

Cammy And what the fuck battlefield skill is that?

Rossco It's the importance ay having a piece ay paper in your hand.

Cammy Very important.

Fraz You should always carry a piece ay paper way you.

Cammy It's fucking crucial tay survival in the modern theatre ay operations.)

Rossco See.

Beat.

I fucking telt you.

Cammy That's a man way seven years' experience you're listening tay there.

Rossco Including a tour ay Kosovo and two tours out here.

Fraz That's the sort ay experience that makes you really appreciate the importance ay having a piece ay paper in your hand.

Cammy Have you got anything written on the piece ay paper?

Rossco I was just getting tay that. It's no actually essential tay hay anything on the paper ay.

Kenzie No?

Rossco It's much more important that you just have the piece ay paper. Either in the hand where it can be seen – (*He demonstrates both moves.*) or tucked away, ready to be whipped out when you're challenged.

Kenzie Will nobody check if there's nothing on it?

Rossco No.

Fraz Not a chance ay anybody checking a piece ay paper.

Cammy A piece ay paper is official.

Rossco See, if you check a piece ay paper, then you might end up having tay day something.

Kenzie Right.

Rossco Cos if you've got time tay be checking some other cunt's bit ay paper then you're obviously no fucking busy enough yerself.

The Sergeant enters.

Sergeant Fucking hell ay. If this is the Quick Reaction Force we're fucked. What the fuck are youse cunts dayin?

Cammy I'm overseeing the fortification ay our living accommodation.

Fraz I'm assisting way the overseeing.

Cammy We wouldnay want tay see luxury like this getting damaged.

Sergeant In my fucking army you cannay oversee fuck all when you've no even got your fucking troosers on.

Fraz We have actually got them on, Sergeant.

Sergeant No you fucking huvnay.

Cammy This is a valuable lesson in keeping hydrated.

Sergeant Hyfuckindrated?

Cammy It's how you . . .

16

Sergeant I fucking ken what fucking hyfuckingdrated fucking means. I just want tay fucking ken how you're sitting on your arse while every other cunt is daying something?

Fraz Firemen.

Sergeant Firefuckingmen?

Cammy Firefuckingmen, Sergeant. Trousers down over the boots. Ready to be jumped into when the alarm goes.

They demonstrate.

Sergeant Fuck's sake.

Cammy I thought the rule was, if the war's a mile away you can relax?

Sergeant The war . . . is over.

Fraz Is it?

Sergeant Aye.

Cammy So what are we doing here?

Sergeant You're here because Her Majesty's Government has decided that there's no way we can sit down in Basra topping up our tans when our allies are getting ten types ay shite knocked out ay them by the *mujahadin*.

Cammy Right. That's it. (*To Fraz.*) We have been wondering about it ay?

Sergeant It's our turn tay be in the shite. But we've had three hundred years ay being in the shite. If you dinnay like shite then you shouldnay have bothered fucking joining.

Beat.

Are you still wanting tay leave when we get back, Campbell?

Cammy Yes, Sergeant.

Sergeant Thank fuck. McKenzie . . . Here . . . Okay. I know I told youse tay listen tay these cunts because they'd been out here before and I thought they kent what the fuck they were dayin . . . but it's fucking official now. This pair, Lance Corporal Campbell here and Private fucking Frazer . . . are a pair ay fannies.

Beat.

What are they?

Kenzie A pair ay fannies.

Sergeant A pair of fannies, Sergeant.

Kenzie A pair of fannies, Sergeant.

Fraz That's a bit harsh.

Sergeant Harsh, ya cunt? My bairns could day a better job.

Beat.

Have you even telt him how much fucking fanny he's gonnay get when he gets home? Have they telt you?

Kenzie No yet, Sergeant.

Sergeant Fucking war heroes, you boys. Who the fuck gets tay say that any more? Million quid?

Beat.

Successful career?

Beat.

I've been in a fucking war, ya cunt. Trumps every cunt. Yous'll be fucking fighting them off. (*Points to Fraz.*) That ugly cunt there even got a fucking ride after we were out here the first time.

Fraz Two.

Sergeant I mean, look at the state ay the cunt.

Beat.

And he came back for more. He fucking left, got bored and came back.

Fraz I wasnay gonnay let these cunts go back tay war wayout me, was I?

Sergeant He realised when else are you ever gonnay get the opportunity tay fire a Milan missile? (*To Fraz.*) You've had that great pleasure though, haven't you?

Fraz Yes, Sergeant.

Sergeant Fired it at a fucking horse and cart.

Fraz It was a donkey and cart.

Sergeant A donkey and cart was taken out at the bargain-basement price ay seventeen thousand, nine hundred and fifty-four quid to the British taxpayer.

Fraz In my defence I thought there was an Iraqi way an RPG in it.

Sergeant Fair do's. But you still spunked twenty grand on turning a donkey intay sandwich paste. Stewarty boy there wrote off a two-million-quid Warrior.

Stewarty (*gives the thumbs up*) That's why they dinnay let me drive anymair.

Sergeant Aye. But when the fuck are any ay you lot ever again, in your whole fucking life, gonnay get the fucking chance tay write off a two-million-quid, state-ay-the-art piece ay kit?

Rossco Never.

Sergeant (*noticing Rossco for the first time*) Fucking never.

Beat.

What are you dayin, Rossco?

Rossco holds up the piece of paper in his hand.

Okay.

Beat.

On you go then.

19

I'm sick ay folk moaning about this deployment.

A mortar lands near by. The Sergeant and the rest of the Soldiers dive for cover.

Get the cards out, then.

There are more explosions.

(*To Kenzie.*) This, this is the best fun you're ever gonnay have. Ever. Where are you fay?

Kenzie Dundee.

Sergeant Well, this is like the Perth Road on a Saturday night. But way airstrikes.

THE GALLANT FORTY-TWA

Sergeant
    Oh it's yinced I wis a weaver
    My name is Willie Brown
    It's yinced I wis a weaver
    I dwelt in Maxwelltoon
    But noo I've joined the sodgers
    And tae Perth I'm going awa
    For tae join that Heilan regiment
    The gallant forty-twa.

All
    Ye can talk aboot your first royals
    Scottish fusiliers
    Your Aiberdeen militia
    And your dandy volunteers
    Your Seaforths wi' their streekit kilts
    And your Gordons big and braw
    But gae bring tae me the tartan
    O' the gallant forty-twa.

    Oh the verra first day on parade
    Was wi' a lot o' young recruits
    And the sergeant he got on tae me

For aye lookin at my boots
He tapped me on the shoulder
Says ye'll hae tae come awa
For you're going tae mak a hell o' a mess
O' the gallant forty-twa.

Ye can talk aboot your first royals
Scottish fusiliers
Your Aiberdeen militia
And your dandy volunteers
Your Seaforths wi' their streekit kilts
And your Gordons big and braw
But gae bring tae me the tartan
O' the gallant forty-twa.

PUB 2

Cammy, Granty and Rossco sit at the table. Macca and Nabsy play pool.

Writer (*getting a tape recorder from his bag*) So when did you join?

Cammy When I was eighteen. I went tay college first. Daying computers, but it was pish. I fucking hated it.

Writer (*to Rossco*) What about you?

Rossco Straight fay school.

Cammy Granty worked for a couple years ay.

Granty But I always wanted to join. My dad just didnay want me tay go when I was sixteen.

Cammy I met him on the way back from the recruiting office and he'd just got his papers.

Granty I was like, fuck college, come awa way me.

Cammy Aye. So I thought, fuck it. I'm gonnay day it.

Granty And we were off.

Cammy Down to Catterick.

Writer What was training like?

Cammy What was training like? Never mind that.

Beat.

What's shagging Sophie like?

Writer What?

Cammy You must be shagging her ay?

Granty Aye.

Rossco Look at the cunt.

Granty Look at his eyes, man.

Cammy Have you shagged her?

Granty You have ay?

Rossco Course he fucking has.

Cammy Is that what you day?

Granty That's what I'd day.

Rossco That's what I'd definitely day.

Cammy D'you get these young lassies tay be researchers and then shag them?

Granty I'll show you how tay be a writer.

Rossco If you chow on this.

Writer I don't really know Sophie that well.

Rossco You dinnay ken her that well?

Writer No.

Granty You've fucked her three ways.

Rossco Every hole in her body.

Granty And you're saying you dinnay ken her that well.

Granty That's fucking bad news like.

Rossco She's gagging on your fucking pole tay get somewhere in life and you fucking blank her in the street?

Writer Look, I think . . .

Granty I would never treat a lassie like that.

Cammy You fucking user cunt.

Granty Are you gonnay use us?

Rossco You are ay?

Writer No.

Granty Cos I dinnay mind like.

Writer You don't?

Granty So long as I get access tay birds like that researcher lassie you're shagging.

Writer Where did you go with the regiment . . . after training?

Cammy Germany.

Granty Fallingbostel.

Rossco We were already over there.

Cammy I liked Germany.

Rossco Aye.

Granty It was good.

Cammy The good life.

Rossco Club 18-30 way rifles.

Granty No as good as Kosovo.

Cammy Kosovo was magic.

Rossco That was just Club 18-30.

Granty Fuck the rifles.

Cammy Every cunt loved us in Kosovo. The Albanians cos we stopped the fighting. The Serbs because we stopped the revenge killings.

Granty We were pissed every night.

Rossco And the fanny's fantastic over there.

Cammy I never saw one fat bird the whole time I was there.

Rossco They're all supermodels.

Granty Apart fay the ones Fraz shagged.

They all laugh.

Writer Is peace-keeping difficult?

Cammy Peace-keeping's harder than war-fighting.

Granty No over there, though.

Rossco All you had tay worry about in Kosovo was the toby tig.

Writer Toby tig?

Rossco It's a game where you wait till someone's daying something.

Granty Changing tracks or a bit of maintenance or sleeping.

Rossco And you go up to them, get your cock out and whack them on the puss way it.

Granty Then they're it.

Rossco And they have to go after someone else way their cock.

Pause.

Writer Any family in the regiment?

Cammy My dad was in it, years ago.

Rossco Nobody.

24

Cammy And my grandad as well. He was at Tobruk, years and years ago.

Granty I had a cousin in the Paras.

Cammy And my great-grandad tay. Years and years and years ago.

Granty Aye, a'right, we fucking get it.

Writer So the history's important?

Granty They drum it intay you fay the first day.

Rossco Fucking non-fucking-stop.

Cammy That's what a regiment is ay? It's history. The Golden Thread. That's what the old timers go on about. It's what connects the past, the present, the future . . .

Writer Is that why you think your grandad joined?

Cammy I dinnay ken.

Rossco He was probably just a fucking idiot tay.)

Granty He's fay a long line ay idiots.

Cammy It was the First World War ay.

Beat.

He volunteered though.

Rossco Every cunt volunteered for the First World War ay.

Granty Nay wonder, they had the recruitment rallies on Saturday nights. In pubs.

Cammy Lord Elgin was the cunt that did them.

Lord Elgin enters with a sword. He places the sword on their table and addresses them.

Lord Elgin Now as you know, my ancestor led his men at Bannockburn and is buried nearby at Dunfermline Abbey. He led his men in a fight for freedom from the tyranny of a

25

foreign power and the need then, as now, for Scotsmen to serve their country in its hour of need is as great.

Beat.

Here on this table in front of me is the sword of my ancestor. The two-handed claymore carried by him on that fateful day six hundred years ago. (*Picks up the sword.*) The sword of Robert the Bruce.

Beat.

I say to you now, as he asked his men that day at Bannockburn, I raise the sword of King Robert the Bruce of Scotland high above my head – (*He does.*) and ask you – (*Shouts.*) wha'll follow a Bruce?

Granty How much?

Lord Elgin What?

Granty How much?

Lord Elgin How much?

Cammy Aye.

Lord Elgin How much?

Rossco Aye.

Lord Elgin This is Robert the Bruce's sword.

Rossco Well, get Robert the fucking Bruce tay go way you then.

Cammy Aye.

Lord Elgin Bannockburn.

Beat.

Freedom.

Beat.

Robert the Bruce and that?

Photographs by Manuel Harlan

6

Granty We're still wanting fucking paid.

Lord Elgin Paid?

Beat.

Fucking paid?

Beat.

Our country faces the gravest peril, the Hun threatens our very civilisation.

Beat.

D'you think you'll be getting fucking paid when the Kaiser bowls up the road and takes over?

Granty Maybe.

Lord Elgin Where do you work, son?

Granty The pit.

Lord Elgin The pit?

Rossco We all day.

Lord Elgin And you dinnay want tay join the army?

Cammy No, we dinnay.

Lord Elgin I mean, come on, it's no just the money. There's the travel.

Granty Travel?

Lord Elgin Aye.

Beat.

Well, France anyway.

Granty France is a'right.

Lord Elgin The fresh air, the meadows, the rivers. The Somme region's fucking beautiful this time ay year . . . You'll no be crouching in an eighteen-inch seam over there.

Granty No?

Lord Elgin Not at all.

Granty That sounds a'right.

Lord Elgin What more do you want? Three square meals a day, games of football way your mates, guns . . .

Rossco We get guns?

Lord Elgin Big fucking guns.

Rossco Guns are fucking magic.

Lord Elgin Guns and football and drink and exotic poontang and that.

Beat.

Shoot a few Germans.

Beat.

You'll have a fucking hoot.

Cammy What about glory?

Lord Elgin Glory?

Cammy Aye?

Lord Elgin Oh aye . . . aye . . . the glory.

Beat.

The glory of returning, at Christmas, a hero.

Beat.

Did I mention it would be all over by Christmas?

Cammy Oh well, when you put it like that.

Granty Aye.

Cammy D'you fancy it?

Rossco Fuck yeah.

Granty I definitely fancy it.

Rossco What the fuck else are we gonnay day?

Granty Aye.

Cammy I cannay be arsed way the pit anymair.

Rossco The pits are fucked.

All Where do we sign?

THE FORFAR SODGER

Lord Elgin
In Forfar I wis born an bred
But faith I div think shame, sir
To tell the weary life I led
Afore I left ma hame, sir.

Hurrah, hurrah
Wi' ma twittle-fal-air-al-aye-doh.

Ma faither wis a weaver poor
Wha ever filled a spool, sir
There never wis beef cam tae the door
But just a pun at Yule, sir.

Hurrah, hurrah
Wi' ma twittle-fal-air-al-aye-doh.

Fan I was six I gaed tae school
Because it wis the fashion
An ilka Sunday tae the kirk
Tae save me o' a thrashin.

Hurrah, hurrah
Wi' ma twittle-fal-air-al-aye-doh.

They learntit me tae read an write
An coont the rule o' three, sir
But a nobler thocht cam tae ma heid
An a sodger I wid be, sir.

Hurrah, hurrah
Wi' ma twittle-fal-air-al-aye-doh.

So I gaed doon tae Forfar toon
'Twas in the Forfar county
An I 'listed there wi' Sergeant Broon
For forty pounds o' bounty.

Hurrah, hurrah
Wi' ma twittle-fal-air-al-aye-doh.

They gied me claes tae hep ma back
An mittens tae ma hands, sir
An swore I wis the brawest cheil
In a' the Heilan clans, sir.

FASHION

(Music. A red carpet rolls out, and as Cammy narrates the
following history of the Black Watch the other soldiers
manoeuvre him around the stage dressing him into and
out of significant and distinct uniforms from the regiment's
history. They resemble a squad assembling and disas-
sembling a military cannon.)   See Picture 1

Cammy We started before Culloden. We dinnay really ken
when. 1715, or maybe 1725. When Scotland was an
independent nation we were fucking mercenaries tay half ay
fuckin Europe. But it was 1739 when we really threw our lot
in way the British.

Beat.

Some people thought we chose this dark tartan tay reflect our
black, betraying hearts. Bollocks.Fuck all that
Cullodenshite.The Highlands were fucked.

Beat.

30

And they let us keep our weapons. Our kilts and our bagpipes. And they told us that we'd never have tay serve abroad. (*Laughs.*) But that's the fucking army for you.

Pause.

So, aye, like I say, formed in 1739. By George the Second. And you can see why they wanted us on the firm ay. We're useful cunts tay hay on board. We're warriors. We're Celts.

Beat.

The thing about the Celts, apart fay being an oral culture and dissapearing fay history, was that they looked upon warfare as sport. It was their fun. It was what they did to relax.

Beat.

Tay us, this . . . this is fucking relaxation.

Pause.

Since 1745 the Black Watch has fought all over the world. A lot ay the time we've been used in tribal conflicts. We're good at them.

Beat.

We're a fucking tribe ourselves.

Beat.

That's why we did so well when they sent us tay the Americas tay fight the Yankees and their Indian allies. They could fight in the forests and so could we.

Beat.

After the American War ay Independence we refused all Battle Honours for our part in it. Because it was rightly decreed that Battle Honours should not be granted for a war with our own kith and kin.

Beat.

I didnay see any cunt I kent. But somebody must ay.

31

Beat.

We've got a lot ay links tay North America. There's a Black Watch in Canada and our Pipes and Drums played at JFK's funeral. They fucking love us over there. Cannay get enough ay the history ay.

Beat.

All the shite they dinnay have.

Pause.

Anyway, after we fought the French and Indians. In America and India. And the French again in Egypt and Portugal and Spain. And at Waterloo in our squares. And somewhere along the way, George the Third decided we deserved tay wear a red vulture feather in our hats.

Beat.

The Red Hackle.

Beat.

We got it for the recapture of two cannons in a little village in Flanders in 1795. Which didnay seem like a big deal at the time. But George the Third must ay thought so.

Beat.

The British Army likes little touches like that. It calls them force multipliers. Gets the cannon fodder hammering down the recruitment office doors.

Pause.

We fought the Russians at Alma. In Crimea. Way our balaclavas on at Balaclava and Sebastopol. Then the Boer War. Which wasnay all that boring. Then off tay France tay fight the Kaiser. Trench foot and mustard gas. And rats. And lice. Where the mud on the bottom ay your greatcoats used tay cut the backs ay your legs, so we'd cut them off above the kilt.

Beat.

32

Mons and Neuve Chapelle, Festubert and Loos. The Somme and Beaumont Hamel. Arras. Wipers. Passchendaele. A hundred battles where more Scotsmen died than ever before. A hundred Cullodens.

Beat.

So fuck Culloden. Again.

Pause.

In the Second World War we were at Dunkirk but we got left behind way the rest ay the Highland Division. We reformed and fought through Sicily and Italy to Monte Cassino. In Burma with the Chindits we fought in Asia which we did again in Korea against the Chinese hordes. We got sent tay Africa tay crush the Mau Mau rebels. We'd been in Africa before of course. At Tobruk and El Alamein in North Africa again. In Egypt, where we'd been in 1917 too. Before we went tay Palestine tay take Jerusalem. Then Syria tay drive out the Ottoman Turks. Which we did in 1919, in Mesopotamia.

Beat.

Mesopotamia?

Beat.

Where the fuck have I heard that before?

Beat.

Oh . . . aye.

Beat.

Here we are.

Beat.

Again.

Fraz, Cammy, Stewarty, Granty, Rossco and Kenzie are watching porn. The Sergeant enters.

Sergeant Fraz. Get that porn off.

Beat.

And get over here.

Fraz joins the Sergeant.

Sergeant What did we discuss earlier?

Fraz Eh . . .

Sergeant (*points into the wagon*) Get that porn down. You dinnay want the Muslim world tuning intay the BBC tay see a load ay porn.

Fraz Yes, Sergeant.

Sergeant And what else did we discuss?

Fraz Sergeant?

Sergeant Do not commit deviant sexual acts in front ay embedded journalists.

Fraz No, Sergeant?

Sergeant And that goes for the lot ay you. Okay.

Beat.

No toby tig in front ay the cameras. The Muslim world will not take kindly to an army whose idea ay recreation is slapping their cocks on each other's pusses.

The Officer enters.

Officer Afternoon, Sergeant Munroe.

Sergeant Afternoon, sir.

Officer Lovely day again.

Sergeant Yes, sir.

Officer Keeping busy, boys?

Sergeant Just getting ready for the embeds, sir.

Officer Sorry about this, boys. One of the hazards of modern warfare.

Beat.

Who's doing the needful?

Sergeant Eh . . . Fraser, Sir.

Officer Really? Your fifteen minutes of fame have finally arrived, have they, Fraser?

Fraz Yes, sir.

What a shame. I mean, what on earth is wrong with a healthy young woman taking a little bit of pride in her appearance, eh, Sergeant Munroe?

Sergeant Nothing, sir.

Officer Absolutely fucking nothing, eh boys?

Fraz What about the cars, sir?

Sergeant The cars are fine.

Fraz Well, they're kinday Granty's porn ay? And we wouldnay want the Muslim world thinking we were here tay steal their petrol for our lovely cars.

Sergeant Good thinking. Take them down then.

Officer Leave them up. Leave it all up.

Sergeant Sir?

Officer It's important that we have a reminder of what we're here fighting for. Porn and petrol. That's a joke by the way, Fraser.

Fraz Yes, sir.

Officer As you were, chaps.

The Officer exits.

Sergeant Take them down.

Fraz But, the officer . . .

Sergeant Get them down. And destroy them.

Fraz Destroy them?

Sergeant Aye.

Fraz But the officer?

Sergeant No arguments.

Beat.

In fact. Fuck it, where's Cammy? Cammy, you're gonnay speak tay the fucking journalists, okay?

Fraz For fuck's sake.

Granty He done it the fucking last time.

Sergeant I dinnay give a fuck. He's daying it again.

Rossco But, I thought it was Fraz's turn?

Sergeant Oh aye, that's really gonnay fucking work ay.

Kenzie One for the housewives?

Sergeant Aye, but what about when he opens his mouth? The boy's a fucking maniac.

Stewarty A good-looking maniac.

Sergeant That cunt, on the fucking six o'clock news?

Beat.

This war's unpopular efuckinough wayout that. (*To Cammy.*) Just smile and reassure the great British public that you are happy in your job.

The Sergeant exits. The Reporter enters with a Cameraman.

Fraz I'm going for a fucking shower. Enjoy.

Granty, Stewarty, Rossco and Kenzie join him.

Reporter Alright?

Cammy A'right.

Reporter Gavin.

Cammy Right.

Cameraman Ric.

Reporter It's Fraser, isn't it?

Cammy Campbell.

Reporter Right . . . Well, we won't keep you long. I'm sure you're probably very busy.

Cammy Aye.

Reporter Have you been with the regiment long?

Cammy Five year.

Reporter Right. Great. (*Pause.*) Have you heard much about all the controversy at home with the amalgamation and everything?

Cammy I dinnay really pay attention tay gossip, mate.

Reporter You're not worried you might lose your job when they disband?

Cameraman Cammy. Can we have you smoking?

Reporter Can we?

Cammy No. Me mum would fuckin kill me.

Reporter So is this your wagon?

Cammy Aye.

Reporter I'm quite impressed – everyone else has porn all over their wagons.

37

Cammy Do they?

Reporter You worry sometimes about the way that must play in the Islamic world?

Cammy Aye.

Beat.

They much prefer it when we're shooting at them.

Cameraman Okay, gang.

Reporter How have you found life here in Camp Dogwood? There's been a lot of controversy at home about the deployment.

Cammy It's a buzz, you're in a war ay, but you're no really doing the job you're trained for but it's no like they're a massive threat tay you or tay your country, you're no defending your country. We're invading their country and fucking their day up.

Reporter Right. Okay. Great. Brilliant. We just need to film that again, but without the swearing.

Cammy Oh. Aye.

Reporter How have you found life here in Camp Dogwood? There's been a lot of controversy at home about the deployment.

There are several explosions. Cammy dives into the back of the wagon. Fraz, Rossco, Kenzie and Granty appear with towels round their waists. Rossco and Granty dive into the back of the wagon. Fraz jumps on the Reporter and Kenzie grabs the Cameraman and points him at Fraz.

Fraz A'right?

Reporter Yes . . . thanks.

Fraz Fraz.

Reporter Gavin.

Beat.

Gav.

Fraz A'right.

Beat.

So . . . Gav . . . you ever been tay Burntisland?

More explosions.

BLUEYS

(Music. Stewarty bursts onto the stage, diving for cover. The door of the Warrior slams shut, isolating him in the space. He lies with his hands over his head as mortars explode around him. The Sergeant enters with a bundle of airmail letters (blueys). Stewarty notices him and takes the letters. He opens one and starts reading it, the words giving him comfort. Another soldier enters and takes the remaining letters. Stewarty creates a subconscious sign-language which expresses the content of his letter. One by one the soldiers enter, take the bundle of letters and, finding the one addressed to them, repeat the process for themselves.   See Picture 2)

ALLIES

Cammy, Fraz, Granty, Rossco, Stewarty, Kenzie, Nabsy and Macca are in the desert. They are watching the horizon which is lit up by a huge bombardment. Airstrikes, helicopters and artillery are pouring fire down. There is a series of massive explosions.

Kenzie These Americans are fucking amazing.

Cammy Do you fucking think so?

Kenzie Aye.

More explosions.

39

Stewarty It's a bit too fucking close for me, like.

Cammy Aye.

Stewarty You ken what these cunts are like ay.

Granty Fucking cowboys.

More explosions.

You kinday feel sorry for the cunts that are stuck in the middle ay that.

Kenzie Day you fuck.

Rossco I hope there's some left over for us.

Kenzie Aye. I want tay get some fucking action at last.

Stewarty Nay cunt'll fucking survive this like.

Nabsy They've been at it for fucking hours.

Macca Four fucking hours.

Rossco There must be fucking hundreds ay the cunts holed up in this place, like.

Fraz They'll be trying tay escape fay Fallujah.

There is the roar of jets overhead and then we see huge bomb explosions.

Cammy This isnay fucking fighting. This is just plain old-fashioned bullying like.

Rossco It's good fun, though.

Cammy D'you think?

Rossco Aye.

Beat.

It's good to be the bully.

Stewarty This is too fucking much though ay?

Cammy Aye. There's just something about these cunts ay.

Fraz Did you see that pair ay fucking knobs that turned up the other day?

Cammy No.

Fraz Two ay their Marines.

Stewarty What a fucking state.

Fraz Pair ay bodybuilder cunts ay.

Stewarty Pair ay fat cunts.

Fraz Their arms were out here.

Granty They were after some kit ay.

Cammy Arseholes.

Granty (*American accent*) 'A tam-o'-shanter.'

Fraz (*American accent*) 'My auntie's Scatch.'

Rossco 'My great grandaddy was in the Black Watch of Scatchland.'

Cammy I hope you telt them tay fuck off.

Granty Fuck that. I got rid ay they two extra, extra, extra, extra large T-shirts.

Fraz And what are you getting.

Granty I'm getting one ay their swanky camp beds off them.

Fraz Aye?

Granty Or cots as I believe they call them.

Cammy The US army field-cot is a luxury model I have to say.

There is another series of huge explosions.

The word is we'll be going out soon.

Fraz Who was telling you that?

Cammy That journalist boy, the day.

Granty Fucking know everything before we do. What did he say?

Cammy He heard that sonics have tracked where all the attacks on the camp are coming from. He reckons the CO's gonnay send a couple of wagons out to see if we can catch the fuckers.

Kenzie I hope it's us he sends.

Macca It's gonnay be fucking dangerous.

Kenzie It's better than sitting here getting mortared all day.

Stewarty You'll no be saying that when we walk into an ambush.

OFFICER EMAIL 2

Yes, my darling, we've heard of little else but the anger that has greeted the news of the amalgamation of the Scottish regiments. And although I find it dispiriting to have the focus of people's ire on the reorganisation, I have to say the Government's timing leaves a lot to be desired. To dissolve the Black Watch during this deployment is bizarre. I heard that Mike Jackson told the *Telegraph* that if these regiments are so precious, why are more young Scotsmen not joining up? I think this might be more to do with the negative perception people have of our current operations back home.

Retired soldiers and officers are criticising the reorganisation because they feel passionately about our history. So do I. But the Black Watch will continue to recruit from Fife and Tayside. We will keep our name, most of our uniform and the Hackle. The essence of the regiment will continue. My main worry is the effect all this fuss could have on the morale of those serving now.

What will happen in the future is a question which should be explored in the future. Were this reorganisation to erode the bonds that connect the regiment to those places which have for the last three hundred years provided the men who make up the Black Watch, then it will be a disaster for both the British Army and the country as a whole. However, as I say, that is a question to which we will no doubt return. At the moment our focus must be on its operations here.

The time has come for peace in the regimental family.

PUB 3

Rossco So, see, what you want tay day ay?

Writer Aye.

Rossco You want tay like show cunts what we fucking done in Iraq?

Writer What you experienced.

Nabsy Will we be getting played by actors?

Writer Well, yes, hopefully, if there's a story.

Granty Who'll be playing me?

Writer It depends.

Granty He better be good-looking, okay.

Macca Get the cunt that was the Elephant Man.

Granty Dinnay fucking dare get the fucking cunt that was the Elephant Man.

Macca Shhhhh . . . my name . . . shhhhh . . . is Private . . . shhhhh Grant.

Granty No. I'm being fucking serious here.

Beat.

It better fucking be some good-looking cunt. Okay?

Writer Okay.

Granty Ewan McGregor. He can be me.

Nabsy (*to Stewarty*) He should be played by that cunt out ay *Dog Soldiers*.

Stewarty Fuck off.

Nabsy The Scottish cunt.

Writer Kevin McKidd?

Nabsy I dinnay ken. The boy way the ginger hair.

Writer Kevin McKidd.

Nabsy The ginger boy.

Stewarty He's no ginger.

Granty Aye he fucking is.

Stewarty Is he fuck.

Nabsy Day they get a lot ay fanny actors?

Writer Yes.

   Beat.

The heterosexual ones at least.

Nabsy Are a lot ay actors poofs like?

Granty Is Ewan McGregor a poof?

Writer No.

Granty He can still be me then.

Nabsy That boy out ay *Dog Soldiers*. The Scottish cunt. He isnay a poof, is he?

Writer I don't think so.

Nabsy No. He's got red hair ay.

Granty I dinnay actually mind if a poof plays me. As long as he's a good-looking poof.

   Beat.

In the Black Watch, the whole Reconnaissance Platoon are poofs.

Writer Are they?

Granty Well, they pretend tay be ay. Just tay freak out all the young cunts.

Pause.

Writer Is it right that in Iraq, during the war you lived in the Warrior?

Cammy The wagon. Aye.

Writer How many soldiers arc in a . . . a wagon?

Granty Three crew.

Cammy Commander.

Granty Driver.

Rossco Gunner.

Stewarty And the dismounts in the back. Five or six ay us.

Rossco And it's fucking tiny.

Cammy It's about the size ay that pool table.

Writer So what was it like living in the back of the wagon for so long?

Stewarty It was alright.

Writer How do you pass the time?

Cammy Slowly.

Rossco Very fucking slowly.

Granty Talking fucking pish.

Cammy You would just end up playing daft wee games. Like name five films that, I dunno, someone's been in.

Writer Who?

Cammy Dunno. Loads ay different cunts ay.

Writer Who?

Cammy Loads ay cunts.

Writer Who?

Granty Ewan McGregor.

Nabsy The boy out ay *Dog Soldiers*. The Scottish cunt. Way the ginger hair.

Stewarty He's no fucking got ginger . . .

Granty And TV programmes tay.

Macca What's your favourite?

Rossco Favourite episodes.

Stewarty Favourite lines and that.

Granty Sometimes we would just have a sing-song.

All
    And it's over the mountains and over the main
    Through Gibraltar, tae France and tae Spain
    Wi' a feather in your bonnet, and a kilt aboon your knee
    Sae list my bonnie laddie and come awa wi' me.

Writer Did you have much contact with Iraqis?

Stewarty I thought you said you were interested in us? I thought it was about our story?

Writer You didn't know any Iraqis?

Stewarty What the fuck have the Iraqis got tay fucking day way anything?

Cammy After the first time, the invasion, it was brilliant. Way the Iraqis. They would totally follow you about the streets, going 'Red Flowers, Red Flowers.'

Granty That's what they called us, cos ay the Hackle ay.

Rossco (*Middle Eastern accent*) 'Red Flowers, Red Flowers. You know David Beckham, Red Flowers?'

Cammy Ya cunt, what fucking country did you fucking invade?

Rossco What?

Granty Was it fucking Wales?

Rossco 'Red Flowers. Red Flowers.'

Macca Pakifuckinstan, ya cunt.

Rossco Hey, any cunt that's got a fucking problem way the accent, we should step the fuck outside for ten seconds and resolve the fucking issue ay?

Cammy I've no got a problem, neebur.

Macca Sound, neebur.

Writer Did you see much of the Americans?

Rossco No really. You tend tay keep out ay their way.

Cammy There was one time we watched them bombing fuck out of this village.

Macca For four fucking hours.

Nabsy There was nay cunt there.

Cammy Nay insurgents, anyway.

Stewarty When we got back tay camp ay, I went and asked a couple ay cunts, what was going on there, last night.

Nabsy We watched them bombing the shite out ay the gaff for fucking ages.

Macca It was fucking mental.

Stewarty They were like, aye, there was nay cunt there, they killed two civilians.

Macca Four hours ay fucking bombing.

47

Cammy Arseholes.

Rossco I mean, it's no like the Iraqis could've fought against us anyway ay.

Granty The difference in the firepower and the kit, it's that much.

Rossco You've got four armoured vehicles somewhere and some bloke jumps out way an RPG?

Stewarty They all blast him.

Rossco He's a fucking idiot.

Writer Did you worry about having to shoot people?

Rossco No if they're firing at you.

Cammy It's nothing tay day way them being Muslims or Arabs or anything.

Rossco I dinnay give a fuck who you are, if you fire a gun at me I dinnay like you. It's nothing personal.

Cammy After the first fire fight we were in, in our wagon, we never spoke or even looked at each other.

Granty We just got on way cleaning the shell-casings out ay the wagon, cleaning the chain gun and that ay.

Cammy It was pretty quiet.

Rossco Then you get used tay it and it's no such a big deal.

Cammy Like I say, way the difference in kit.

　　Beat.

After a while, it's more bullying than fighting ay.

Stewarty You dinnay join up tay bully cunts day you.

Rossco Bullying's the job.

Granty It's no the reason you want tay be in the army, though.

Cammy It's a buzz, you're in a war ay, but you're no really doing the job you're trained for but it's no like they're a massive threat tay you or tay your country, you're no defending your country. We're invading their country and fucking their day up.

TWA RECRUITING SERGEANTS

Fraz *and* **Kenzie**
There was twa recruiting sergeants came frae the Black Watch
Through markets and fairs, some recruits for tae catch
But a' that they listed was forty and twa
Sae list my bonnie laddie and come awa.

For it's over the mountain, over the main
Through Gibraltar, tae France and tae Spain
Wi' a feather in your bonnet and a kilt aboon your knee
Sae list my bonnie laddie and come awa wi' me.

O laddie ye dinna ken the danger that yer in
If yer horses wis tae fleg and yer owsen wis tae rin
This greedy ole farmer, he wouldna pay yer fee
Sae list my bonnie laddie and come awa wi' me.

For it's over the mountain, over the main
Through Gibraltar, tae France and tae Spain
Wi' a feather in your bonnet and a kilt aboon your knee
Sae list my bonnie laddie and come awa wi' me

O laddie if ye've got a sweetheart an bairn
Ye'll easily get rid o' that ill-spun yarn
Twa rattles o' the drum and that'll pay it a'
Sae list my bonnie laddie and come awa.

All
For it's over the mountain, over the main
Through Gibraltar, tae France and tae Spain
Wi' a feather in your bonnet and a kilt aboon your knee
Sae list my bonnie laddie and come awa wi' me.

(Stewarty, Nabsy and Macca enter and join Fraz and Kenzie.
They climb on the pool table and the baize surface sinks
under their feet. The soldiers sit around the edge of the
table as if in the back of a Warrior.   See Picture 3)

ON PATROL

Kenzie It's fucking hot.

Fraz Hot?

Kenzie Aye.

Fraz Fucking hot?

Kenzie Aye.

Fraz You dinnay ken the meaning ay fucking hot. Ay
Stewarty?

Stewarty You're fucking lucky it's no the fucking summer.

Fraz Sixty fucking degrees in here it was.

Stewarty Fifty outside, sixty in here.

Fraz Stuck for fucking days on fucking end. Hatches shut.

Stewarty Some boys didnay even have desert kit. There was
ammo cooking off in the guns and shooting folk.

Fraz Cannay get out in case you get mortared. Snipers
everywhere.

   Beat.

That was war fighting.

Nabsy Is it true?

Fraz Is what fucking true?

Nabsy What the Sergeant said. We get loads ay fanny after?
When we go back?

Fraz I always gets loads ay fanny.

Stewarty Day you fuck.

Fraz Aye, I fucking day.

Stewarty Ugliest cunt in the regiment.

Fraz I tell you what you day get, though.

Nabsy What?

Fraz Loads ay stupid fucking questions. Isn't that right, Stewarty?

Stewarty (*high-pitched voice*) 'You werc in Iraq?'

Fraz 'Aye. I was.'

Stewarty 'What was it like?'

Fraz 'It was alright.'

Stewarty 'But . . . did you like . . . see anything?'

Fraz 'No. I kept my eyes shut for the whole six months.'

Stewarty 'Did you kill anyone?'

Fraz 'I lost count at twenty-three, darlin.'

Kenzie I cannay wait till I get tay shoot some cunt.

Fraz Just make sure it isnay one of us.

Kenzie D'you think there'll fucking be any fighting today?

Fraz Aye.

Kenzie Aye?

Fraz Definitely.

Kenzie Definitely?

Stewarty We're going tay raid the village all they fucking mortars are coming from and you're asking if there's gonna be fighting?

Fraz And we've got our fucking helmets on.

Stewarty Helmet, fighting.

Beat.

Fraz Tam-o'-shanter Hearts and Minds.

Stewarty Helmets, they'll be mortars, snipers . . .

Fraz TOS, you're gonnay hay a game ay fitba way their bairns.

Kenzie I'm no playing fitba way some cunt that's trying tay kill me.

Fraz Aye you fucking are.

Beat.

And you'll let the little cunts fucking win tay.

There is a large explosion outside the wagon.

Cammy Contact.

Stewarty What?

Cammy The other wagon's been hit.

Fraz What the fuck was it, mortars?

Cammy IED bud. Front tracks. They've radioing 'mobility kill'.

Fraz Any cunt hurt?

Cammy They're all fine.

Granty Bumps and lumps and peppered tweeds.

Cammy Right. We're going in tay fucking pick them up.

Kenzie Let's fucking go, come on.

Fraz Shut the fuck up.

Kenzie Fuck you.

There is a blast outside the wagon. The Dismounts are thrown around in the back by both the blast and the movement of the wagon as it starts to move. The shouts of the crew come across the battlenet into the back.

Cammy Traverse right!

Granty Reverse right?

Cammy Traverse right!

Granty I am reversing right!

Cammy Traverse! Traverse, you cunt! Watch the fucking ditch!

The wagon lurches around. There is another explosion. The Dismounts are piled in the centre of the wagon in a heap. The wagon comes to a halt.

Cammy Is everybody alright?

Stewarty Aye.

Fraz What the fuck's happenning?

Rossco Mortars.

Granty I cannay move it, Cammy. We're fucking stuck.

Fraz He told you to watch the fucking ditch.

Kenzie Let's fucking go.

Stewarty Sit fucking down. We've been hit. We're going nowhere.

TEN-SECOND FIGHTS

Kenzie Cheese on toast.

Stewarty Cheese on fucking toast?

Kenzie Aye.

Fraz You cannay hay cheese on fucking toast.

Kenzie How fucking no?

Nabsy Cos you cannay.

Kenzie How no?

Fraz It's no a fucking Indian, is it?

Kenzie It's fucking food.

Macca It's no a fucking Indian.

Kenzie We're talking about food you want when you get home.

Stewarty Indian fucking food.

Kenzie I just want cheese on fucking toast, okay.

Fraz You cannay have cheese on fucking toast.

Kenzie Aye, I can.

Nabsy You cannay.

Kenzie That's the first thing I'm having soon as I get back.

Fraz Fucking fanny.

Stewarty Chinky?

Fraz Black bean king prawn.

Stewarty Lemon chicken.

Fraz Sweet and sour chicken.

Stewarty You've already had a fucking go.

Fraz I like chinkys. Crispy beef.

Stewarty One fucking go each. Nabsy.

Nabsy Vegetarian sweet and sour.

Fraz Are you a vegetarian like?

Nabsy No.

Fraz Are you sure?

Kenzie You need tay eat some fucking meat.

54

Stewarty Okay. Macca.

Macca Deep fried king prawn roll. Sesame prawn toast. Pickled ginger duck chow mein. Fried rice. Chips. Sweet and sour sauce. Dim sum dipper. Prawn crackers.

Beat.

Two prawn crackers.

Stewarty Fuck's sake. Kenzie.

Kenzie Cheese on toast.

Fraz hits Kenzie on the head. Nabsy laughs.

Kenzie (*to Nabsy*) What are you fucking laughing at?

Nabsy Shut your fucking puss, you fucking prick.

Kenzie Fuck you, ya cunt.

Nabsy What?

Kenzie You think I'm fucking scared ay you?

There is a brief scuffle. Fraz pulls them apart.

Fraz You pair ay fucking stupid cunts.

Sergeant Have we got a fucking problem here?

Fraz No, we fucking haven't.

Sergeant You fucking two.

Beat.

Ten fucking seconds.

They all get out of the wagon. Kenzie and Nabsy remove their helmets and square up to each other.

Sergeant Fraz.

Fraz Ten.

Kenzie and Nabsy tear into each other. Kicking and punching, they fall to the floor.

Nine.

Pause.

Eight.

Pause.

Seven.

Pause.

Music. The soldiers all pair up around the space and attack each other in turn, each fight lasting exactly ten seconds, as the video screens count down from ten to one. The music, movement and countdowns intensify to a climax.

See Picture 4

Six. (*Long pause.*) Five. (*Very long pause.*) Four.

Sergeant Three. Two. One.

The rest of the Dismounts pull Kenzie and Nabsy apart.

Sergeant What are you daying?

Fraz That wasnay a bad fight.

Sergeant Fuck off. It was shite.

Beat.

I had tay stop it before one ay them came. Get fucking up and shake fucking hands. That's the fucking end ay it. Okay.

Kenzie and Nabsy shake.

Sergeant Next time you'll be fighting me. And you dinnay fucking want tay be daying that.

Cammy So what's happening?

Sergeant The other wagon's fucked. We're gonnay hay tay wait till they get a transport down here tay pick it up.

Cammy How long's that gonnay be?

Sergeant Who the fuck knows, Cammy.

Cammy We're sitting fucking ducks out here. That road's got fucking . . .

Sergeant Aye, I ken about the road.

Beat.

Tell me something I dinnay ken.

Granty Fraz is a pre-op transexual.

Sergeant Something I dinnay ken.

Beat.

Right. Get a perimeter set up, Cammy. (*Beat.*) Fraz, Kenzie, come way me. We're going up tay the road way the translator. Stop and search some ay this fucking traffic. You never ken what might turn up. They've had plenty ay time tay get organised. We might as well be some fucking use tay some cunt while we're stuck here.

The Dismounts begin to gather their kit.

Sergeant Right. Let's fucking go.

OFFICER EMAIL 3

My darling, there was a lot of talk as we were moved up from the south that we wouldn't be in any more danger that we had been. This isn't the case. We now face an enemy different to any we've faced in the regiment's history.

(And whilst the insurgents, like the IRA before them, are *Excluded from* particularly adept at vehicle-borne improvised explosive *performance.* devices, we have never had to face an enemy intent on delivering them suicidally.)

This is the main concern. I know it unsettles the boys. And they are for the most part boys, when we get hold of them, although they have to grow up quickly out here. The suicide-

57

bombers are recruited as boys too, by all accounts. Makes you think about why they do it.

We in the West have failed to understand the logic of suicide terrorism. The choice to become a religious martyr is the outcome of a struggle to establish an identity in adolescence. The possibility of death, once accepted, presents an alternative idea of the self as a religious warrior. They're looking for glory, and they seem to be finding it in martyrdom. Glory, however, is something which my boys are very unlikely to emerge with. The controversy around this war means there'll be no victory parade for us.

Once again, for those further up the chain of command, to expect troops to be able to adapt to this very, very new situation in a very short space of time is asking a great deal. We face an extremely experienced, well-trained and often very, very dedicated people and it's hardly surprising that they are trying to get at us as soon as they can.

I suspect this may turn into a battle of wills.

PUB 4

See Picture 6

Writer What's it like when you're attacked?

Cammy It's not as bad as you think ay. I mean it's not like you think about it ay.

Granty The training just kicks in.

Writer And does the training work?

Nabsy Well, it must do ay.

Macca I mean, we're still fucking here ay.

Stewarty We're no all fucking here.

Writer What was it like getting fired at?

Cammy It's weird ay.

Stewarty It fucks people up. Big time.

Beat.

Rips them apart.

Beat.

You seen the size ay the bullets we use in a chain gun?

Beat.

You seen what happens when a bullet that size hits somebody?

Writer Well . . . no . . . I haven't.

Stewarty So how the fuck are you gonnay explain it tay folk, then?

Pause.

Writer Did you keep a count?

Stewarty A count?

Writer Of the people you killed. Among yourselves. On the wagon?

Rossco We'd have run out ay fucking room ay.

Stewarty Why d'you want tay ken about a count?

Nabsy Some people kept counts, scratched stuff on lighters, or went about saying 'How many have you got?'

Stewarty What the fuck has that got tay day way anything?

Rossco I never bothered ay.

Granty Aye you fucking did.

Rossco I fucking never.

59

Stewarty (*to the Writer*) Is this what you want tay day ay?

Macca (*to Rossco*) Aye, you did.

Rossco I never.

Stewarty (*to the Writer*) You want tay get off on folk having tay kill cunts?

Nabsy (*to Rossco*) You fucking did.

Rossco I never. (*To the Writer.*) I lost count at twenty-three.

Stewarty You ken what this cunt wants tay day ay?

Cammy What's that, pal?

Stewarty This cunt wants tay make a name for himself by telling every cunt how we're all a fucking shower ay cunts.

Cammy Is that what he's doing?

Stewarty Aye.

Cammy (*to the Writer*) Is that what you're daying?

Writer No –

Stewarty That's how these cunts day it though ay?

  Beat.

They're only fucking interested if they think they're gonnay get some fucking dirt on you.

Cammy Well, that's what the public want ay?

Writer Usually.

Cammy He's just daying his job, Stewarty.

Stewarty And we were just daying our fucking job.

Writer (*to Stewarty*) I understand that.

Stewarty No you fucking dinnay.

  Beat.

See if he wants tay see what it's like to kill some cunt?

Beat.

What we should do is have a few more drinks.

Beat.

Then we can go out and find some cunt and kick them tay death.

Rossco (*stands up*) Stewarty, maybe you and me should go and hay a fag ay?

Cammy Aye. That's a good idea.

Rossco Macca?

Rossco, Macca and Stewarty leave.

Cammy Dinnay worry about him ay.

Granty He's got depression.

Cammy He had tay get bugged out ay.

Granty After a couple ay boys we kent got killed.

Cammy Some boys didnay take it too good ay.

Writer I understand.

Cammy You dinnay.

Beat.

But dinnay worry about it.

Granty See, if you want sick stuff, you should interview a few tankies like.

Nabsy Pure fucking sadists, they cunts.

Granty Mind that time we were in fucking Az Zubayr and we got the tankies to clear that fucking cunt we saw way the RPG?

Nabsy It was Stewarty that got them tay day it.

Granty We were oot the wagon ay and Stewarty said tay the tankies, 'There's a cunt up in this winday, you want tay get rid ay him for us?'

Nabsy He was on his own but he was being a pain in the arse ay.

Granty We thought they would just use the fifty cal ay. They used a fucking HES round ay.

Nabsy Fucking uranium-tipped.

Granty It was only one fucking cunt.

Nabsy Fucking vaporised him.

Granty The fucking building. The five buildings behind it.

Nabsy Fuck knows how many cunts were in them.

Granty Stewarty went mental ay. He got one ay them after, what the fuck did you use a HES round for? This cunt does nay give a fuck ay. He just shrugs and goes, 'Oh, we needed tay change the fucking round anyway.'

Stewarty, Rossco and Macca enter.

Writer What was it like when one of you got killed?

Cammy Well, when something like that happens the Pipe Major goes and plays on the spot where it happened.

Writer No, I mean what is it like when it actually happens? At the time?

Granty Well, it's weird ay cos you've got a zap number.

Writer A zap number?

Cammy It's your first initials ay your second name, and your number. I was CA, Charlie Alpha, four, four, zero, two.

Granty So when something happens, it comes over the radio way the zap number ay the folk involved and then the code.

Cammy P-one, walking wounded. P-two wounded. P-three immediate surgery. P-four dead or dying.

Granty You hear the zap number and the codes and you're trying tay think who the fuck is that?

Rossco And the boys that are injured, they'll be changing all the time too ay.

Nabsy They can go fay P-three tay P-four in like ten seconds.

Stewarty That's what happened tay Fraz, Kenzie and the Sergeant.

Granty When we got done by the suicide-bomber.

Macca They done it clever like.

Nabsy Lured us in.

Cammy IED'd the first wagon.

Rossco Mortared us.

Writer IED?

Cammy Improvised explosive device.

Macca They must have been watching us the whole time.

Rossco I seen the car coming. We were on a road ay. So there's gonnay be the occasional car.

Granty We were stuck there too long.

Cammy They had plenty time tay get a suicide-bomb together and get down there.

Rossco We'd never had tay deal way a suicide-bomb before.

Cammy Fraz, Kenzie and the Sergeant had gone up tay speak tay the cunt ay.

Granty Way the translator.

Cammy There was a translator, an Iraqi boy, he was on the other wagon, the one that broke down.

Writer What was his name?

Granty They didnay use their real names.

63

Cammy Tay protect their families from getting in the shite. For working for us.)

Macca He died tay.

Writer Did anyone else get hurt?

Stewarty I broke my arm.

Writer Did you?

Stewarty Sierra Tango two, two, four, five.

Beat.

P-two.

Writer Walking wounded?

Stewarty Walking fucking wounded. See when it got better. My arm. I fucking broke it again myself. (*Pause.*) And I kept breaking it.

Beat.

It would get better and I would break it myself.

Beat.

Get better. Break it myself.

Beat.

Better. Break it.

Beat.

Better. Break it.

Beat.

Better.

Beat.

Break it. (*Pause.*) Write that down.

Writer I will.

Stewarty Write it down way a broken arm though.

Stewarty grabs the Writer's arm.

Cammy Come on Stewarty, leave the boy alone.

Stewarty Let me break your arm and see if you can write it down way a broken arm.

Cammy Stewarty, come on tay fuck.

Stewarty If he wants tay ken about Iraq, he has tay feel some pain?

Cammy It's no his fault.

They pull Stewarty away from the Writer.

Stewarty Fuck off.

Cammy and the Writer are left alone.

You a'right?

Writer Yes.

Cammy You sure?

Writer I'm fine. Thanks for stepping in.

Cammy I knew it was gonnay be a fucking disaster, you coming here . . .

Writer Is he always like that?

Cammy Stewarty was signed off with depression after we got back from Iraq the first time. But when they knew they were going back they lost his paperwork. No just his. Everycunt who'd tried to leave. Stewarty shouldn't have been there the second time.

Writer That's awful.

Cammy If they need you they'll lose your paperwork.

Writer No, I mean to have to go back, when he wasn't . . . mentally . . . ready.

Cammy If you cannay take a joke, dinnay join.

Writer Did a lot of people leave with you?

Cammy Well, every cunt left that was in here the night. Half the fucking regiment must ay fucked off in the end.

Writer It must be terrible seeing your friends die.

Cammy I'm no out ay the army cos ay anything like that.

Writer No?

Cammy It was fuck all tay day way what happened. People getting killed is part ay it ay.

Writer So what was it?

SUICIDE

The wagon is parked beside the road.

Rossco When the fuck are they coming tay get us?

Cammy I dinnay ken.

Rossco I'm fucking dying for a fucking shite like.

Nabsy Aye, me tae.

Cammy Shut up and keep an eye on the road. You're supposed tay be covering them.

Rossco I'm fucking touching cloth here.

Cammy Anything on the net, Granty?

Granty Nothing, mate.

Cammy Fucking Yank pricks, man. If it was any ay their cunts stuck out here they'd be fucking picked up quick enough.

Stewarty Fuck's sake.

Cammy What is it?

66

Stewarty Fucking Fraz, man.

Rossco What's he daying?

Stewarty Terrorising the innocent motorists ay Iraq. Him and the translator.

Granty Fraz doesnay need a translator.

Rossco Does he fuck.

Cammy You jump in the car way the wife and family for a bit ay a drive and the next thing you know that cunt's in the winday quizzing you about the nearest disco.

Rossco His patter's murder tay like.

Granty He'll be slavering some pish.

Cammy He'll be claiming he kens them.

Rossco 'I ken you.'

Beat.

'I day.'

Beat.

'I day.'

Cammy He'll be trying tay pull some poor lassie.

Macca At least he's daying something, Kenzie's standing about like a spare prick.

Granty He hasnay got a fucking clue, that cunt.

Rossco And the Sergeant's channelling his inner traffic warden. Hang on. I think they've found something in this cunt's car.

Granty I hope it's porn.

They all laugh. There is a massive explosion from the road.

*

(Music. The Sergeant, Fraz and Kenzie are propelled into
the air by the blast wave. They fall to the ground one by
one during the following voice-over, as if in slow motion.)
See Picture 5

Voice-Over Mother Uniform, three, three, six, two.

Beat.

P-four.

Kilo Echo, five, five, zero, two.

Beat.

P-four.

Foxtrot Romeo, five, five, six, one.

Beat.

P-three.

Foxtrot Romeo five, five, six, one.

Beat.

P-four.

THE FUTURE

Cammy is mopping up blood.

Officer Campbell.

Cammy How are you, sir?

Officer Well . . . I'd complain, but who'd fucking listen? You
could have got someone else to do that.

Cammy I didnay want it tay upset any ay the boys that werenay there ay. No if we're going back out.

Officer Well, we think we know where they are.

Cammy Good.

Officer And we owe them after today. You know, it would be okay if you didn't go.

Cammy I'm going, sir. This could be my last chance.

Officer It could be the regiment's last chance.

Cammy Maybe. But I know it's mine. I've fought my war.

Beat.

I'm going hame tay bore every cunt in the pub tay death.

Officer So you're thinking about leaving us?

Cammy Absofuckinglutely sir. I'm offski.

Officer You did really well today. Getting those wounded lads out of there.

Cammy Did I?

Officer You're going to get stuck up for a medal for that today. You're the type of man this regiment needs, Campbell.

Cammy We're no gonnay be this regiment any more.

Officer I had you down as a Company Sergeant Major.

Cammy Well, if I can speak frankly, sir?

Officer Go ahead.

Cammy Maybe your judgement's a bit off.

Officer Well . . . you might be right . . . but not about you.

Cammy I enjoyed the war fighting, sir. I really did. That's why I didn't get out after the last tour, sir. I thought, I've got to give it a fucking chance. But this isnay the job, is it, sir?

Officer It's all the job.

Cammy This is pish. Sitting about daying camp security. Getting mortared all the time. Getting fucking ambushed. Getting killed by suicide-bombers. And for what?

    Beat.

My mind's made up.

Officer Fair enough.

Cammy Can I ask you something, sir?

Officer Ask away.

Cammy Well . . . you ken, I thought I kent why I was here. I really couldnay ever have seen myself behind the deli counter in Tesco or anything like that. I always wanted tay be a soldier. And this is way all due respect, sir . . .

    Beat.

What the fuck are you doing here?

Officer What am I doing here?

Cammy Yes, sir.

Officer Well, I'm . . . I'm . . . what's the word . . .

    Pause.

Cursed.

Cammy Cursed, sir?

Officer Yeah. Cursed. You see . . . my father, he was in Korea. Nineteen years old, Second Lieutenant. Got wounded. And promoted. And his father, he was at Loos. And his father, well he was more of a gambler than anything else, but you get my drift.

Cammy I think so, sir.

Officer Some of us . . . It's in the blood.

70

Beat.

And I always thought . . . well, it's not like any other job, is it?

Beat.

(It's part of who we are, where we come from. It's the reason you join up in the first place. The Golden Thread.

Cammy People have said that about a lot of things. The shipyards, the pits. They can have all the adverts they want, but if cunts like me are sacking it, it's . . .

Officer It's a fucking shame.

Cammy It's fucking knackered. Don't you think it's knackered, sir?

Officer It takes three hundred years to build an army that's admired and respected around the world. But it only takes three years pissing about in the desert in the biggest western foreign policy disaster ever to fuck it up completely.)

Beat.

But you didn't hear that from me.

Beat.

We could be off to Afghanistan next. It's going to be exactly the same. Kandahar. Helmand province. It's the only place on the planet that might be slightly more dangerous than here.

The noise of an explosion.

Officer We're going to be hearing that noise for years to come.

Cammy Not me, sir.

Officer No.

Cammy No.

The Officer leaves.

Scotland always had people willing tay serve in the army.

Nabsy I dinnay ken what it was.

Stewarty It must be because we were fucking stupid or something ay.

Rossco We just love fucking fighting.

Macca It was the regimental system ay. It was perfect.

Granty You got tay go way the people you kent.

Rossco And you get to fight.

Nabsy That's what we're trained for.

Cammy That's what we joined the army tay day.

Rossco Fight.

Cammy No for our government.

Macca No for Britain.

Nabsy No even for Scotland.

Cammy I fought for my regiment.

Rossco I fought for my company.

Granty I fought for my platoon.

Nabsy I fought for my section.

Stewarty I fought for my mates.

Cammy Fucking shite fight tay end way though.

Officer This may be the last attack for the First Battalion, the Black Watch. Let us make sure it goes as well as anything we have done in the past and is one that we can be proud of.

Pause.

Five – four – three – two – one.

Beat.

Forward the Forty-Second!

PARADE

(Music. The bagpipes and drums start playing 'The Black Bear'. The soldiers start parading. The music intensifies and quickens as the parade becomes harder and the soldiers stumble and fall. The parade formation begins to disintegrate but each time one falls they are helped back onto their feet by the others. As the music and movement climax, a thunderous drumbeat stops both, and the exhausted, breathless soldiers are left in silhouette.)

See Pictures 7 and 8